T0381380

God's Love

Amya Penny Anysia Turpin

Illustrations By: Amya Penny Anysia Turpin
And Barbara Ann Mary Mack

AuthorHouse™
1663 Liberty Drive
Bloomington, IN 47403
www.authorhouse.com
Phone: 833-262-8899

Because of the dynamic nature of the Internet, any web addresses or links contained in this book may have changed
since publication and may no longer be valid. The views expressed in this work are solely those of the author and do not
necessarily reflect the views of the publisher, and the publisher hereby disclaims any responsibility for them.

Any people depicted in stock imagery provided by Getty Images are models,
and such images are being used for illustrative purposes only.
Certain stock imagery © Getty Images.

This book is printed on acid-free paper.

ISBN: 978-1-4567-2750-5 (sc)

Library of Congress Control Number: 2011901719

Print information available on the last page.

Published by AuthorHouse 10/22/2024

authorHOUSE®

<u>ACKNOWLEDGMENTS</u>

AMYA EMAILS HER PUBLISHING CONSULTANT (AIMEE REFF) A
NOTE OF GRATITUDE.

Thank You Life
(GOD)!

Thank you Niki
Manbeck for your
help!

Hi Madelyn
Lee and
Amanda Lee

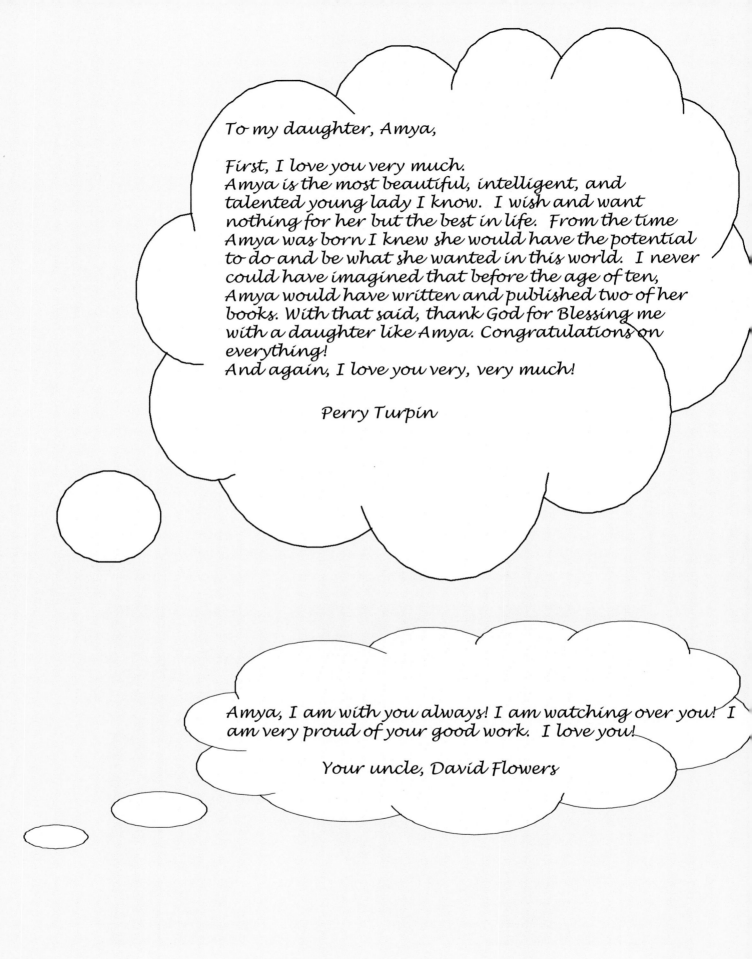

To my daughter, Amya,

First, I love you very much.
Amya is the most beautiful, intelligent, and
talented young lady I know. I wish and want
nothing for her but the best in life. From the time
Amya was born I knew she would have the potential
to do and be what she wanted in this world. I never
could have imagined that before the age of ten,
Amya would have written and published two of her
books. With that said, thank God for Blessing me
with a daughter like Amya. Congratulations on
everything!
And again, I love you very, very much!

Perry Turpin

Amya, I am with you always! I am watching over you! I
am very proud of your good work. I love you!

Your uncle, David Flowers

To God,

I thank You Lord for using Amya to share Your Words of Love to Your children of all ages around the world. Our family is truly "Blessed" to know You, and work for You!

To The Readers,

Amya is not more special or loved more by God because of the books He has given her to write. Amya is like most other kids.
She hates going to school and getting up early for Church. She loves watching TV and playing with her friends. She can't wait until she can walk to the corner store by herself. Amya is "Proof" that God chooses ordinary people to tell His Words to His flock. God Loves all people! You, the reader are "Special in God's Eyes" too, because He has called you into His Kingdom through this book.

To Amya,

I love you very much! And I enjoy spending time with my little thing (Amya). I am very proud of the kindness and generosity that you show to people.
You have definitely been a major positive influence on my life. You make me try to be a better Christian and person, because I know that I have to be an example for you. Let's both try to keep up the good work together!

Mommy

PROLOGUE

HUMAN BEINGS CAME FROM "THE ESSENCE OF LOVE" (ALMIGHTY GOD).
HUMAN BEINGS ARE GOD'S GREATEST CREATION!
WE DID NOT COME FROM A MYSTERIOUS ORIGIN SUCH AS
THE BIG BANG THEORY, EVOLUTION, OR A CAUSE AND EFFECT
OCCURENCE:
WE (HUMAN BEINGS) WERE CREATED BY OUR "DIVINE CREATOR
AND GOD":
THE INHABITANTS OF EARTH WERE CREATED BY "ALMIGHTY GOD":
AMYA'S BOOK, WHICH WAS GIVEN TO HER FROM ALMIGHTY GOD
DECEMBER 31, 2009, LETS THE READERS KNOW OF GOD'S TRUE
EXISTENCE AND PRESENCE IN OUR LIVES TODAY!
THE REALITY OF ALMIGHTY GOD AS "THE ORIGIN" AND
"CREATOR" OF ALL LIFE IS EXPRESSED THROUGHOUT AMYA'S
BOOK.
THE REALITY OF GOD BEING "THE BEGINNING OF LIFE", GIVES HIS
CHILDREN OF ALL AGES THE COMFORT OF KNOWING THE LOVING
CREATOR (GOD) OF ALL LIFE.
GOD CREATED BABIES, LITTLE BOYS AND GIRLS, MOMS AND DADS,
PETS AND FRIENDS, PLANTS AND TREES:
HE CREATED MOUNTAINS AND THE GREAT WATERS (SEAS, OCEANS
AND RIVERS) AND THE LIFE WITHIN THEM.
GOD CREATED EVERYTHING THAT IS GOOD AND HOLY SO THAT WE
MAY ENJOY EVERYTHING THAT COMES FROM HIM.
GOD CREATED EVERYTHING THAT IS GOOD! GOD CREATED LIFE!

THE WORDS THAT ARE WRITTEN WITHIN THE "CALLOUTS" WERE
GIVEN TO AMYA FROM ALMIGHTY GOD ON DECEMBER 31, 2009,
AND JANUARY 1, 2010.

> BARBARA ANN MARY MACK
> (AMYA'S GRANDMOM)

LIFE

AMYA SPEAKING TO GOD'S CHILDREN:

Lord God made life! He made you and me.

AMYA, MOMMY (LATOYA) AND GRANDMOM (BARBARA)

AMYA AND DADDY

JAMES AND AMYA AFTER SCHOOL

God is the One to thank! We should praise and thank Him for Life!

FUN OUTSIDE WITH JABRIL AND HIS BROTHER JAHAD

LIFE (BIRDS) IN THE AIR AND ON THE GROUND

Birdies By:
Barbara Ann Mary Mack
October 26, 2010

BREAKFAST TIME

AMYA AND GRANDMOM SWINGING AT THE PLAYGROUND

AMYA HAVING FUN AT THE PLAYGROUND

AMYA RIDES HER SCOOTER

HE IS THE MASTER OF LIFE.

AMYA FEEDS HER CAT (KITTY) HIS FAVORITE FOOD

He breathed us into existence!
God wanted us to live on this Earth!

We are so happy to be able to live on Earth!

Thank You Lord for Life! The Lord gave us life!

BABY AIDEN (AMYA'S NEXT DOOR NEIGHBOR)
ENJOYS HIS AFTERNOON SNACK

SUGAR (AMYA'S DOGGIE) AND HER TOY BONE

LIFE (FISH AND MANY PLANTS) WITHIN THE WATERS
(PICTURE OF THE SUSQUEHANNA RIVER)

HAPPY HALLOWEEN

AMYA (A FAIRY) AND MUMMY (MOMMY) HALLOWEEN 2010.
TRICK OR TREAT! AMYA AND HER FAMILY LOVE TO DRESS UP FOR
HALLOWEEN.

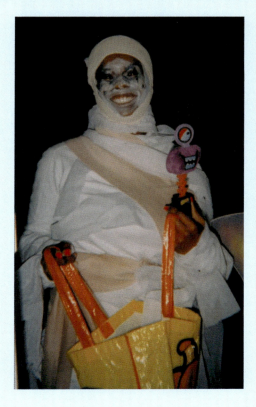
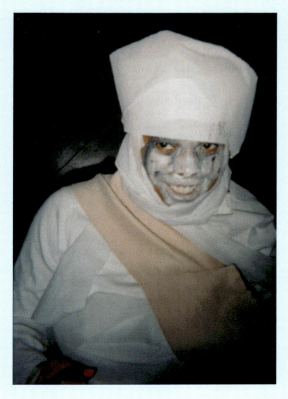

GRANDMOM, AS MARY (*JESUS'* MOTHER)
AND AMYA, A BEAUTIFUL FAIRY

AMYA AND HER MOM EXAMINE THEIR GOODIES AFTER
TRICK OR TREATING IN THE NEIGHBORHOOD.

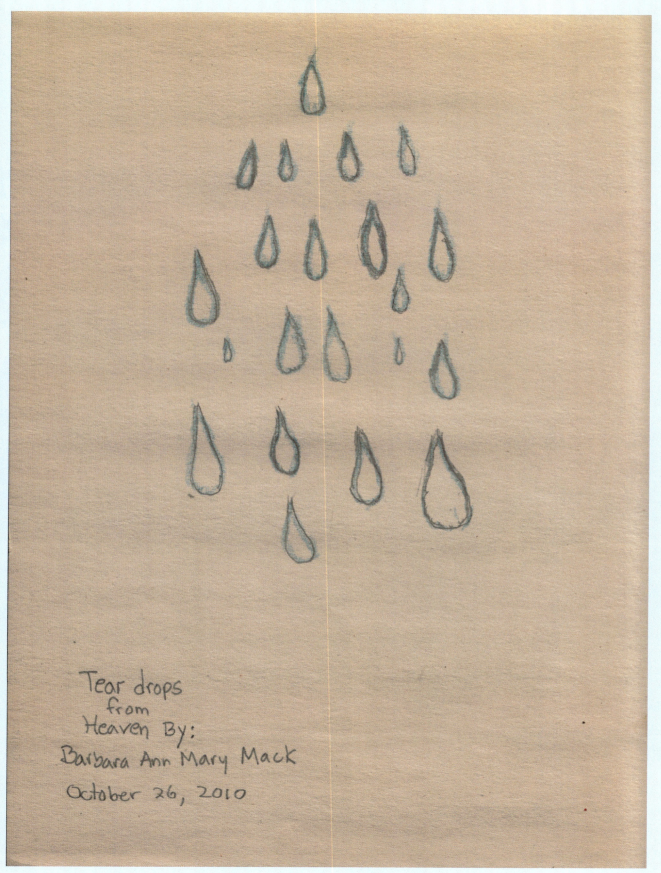

Tear drops
    from
Heaven By:
Barbara Ann Mary Mack
October 26, 2010

Father, do You ever cry? If You do, don't, because I'm here!

AMYA AND GOD'S TEARS (RAINDROPS)

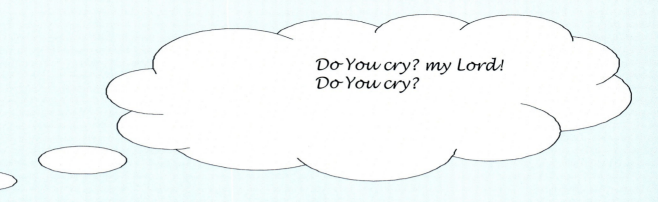

GOD'S FALLING TEARS (RAIN DROPS)

GOD'S TEARS (RAIN) HELP PLANTS AND TREES GROW (GRANDMOM'S LIMA BEAN PLANTS)

Do You cry at night when the moon is shining bright?

If You do, don't! Because I'm here.

Drawing of Amya and Jesus

Amya Turpin

Jesus crying

Amya helping him

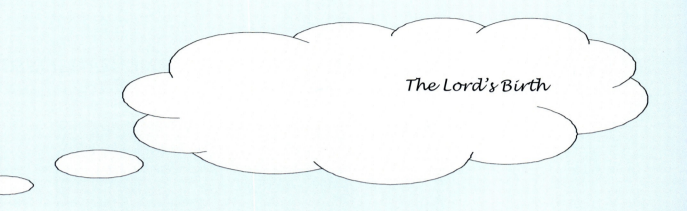

The Lord's Birth

The Lord was born on Christmas.   God gave His Only Son to save us from sin. Jesus was so special: He got gifts on His Birthday!

GRANDMOM MACK IS MAKING THE CROWN AND MANGER SCENE FOR BABY *JESUS* (using one of Amya's dolls and toy animals).

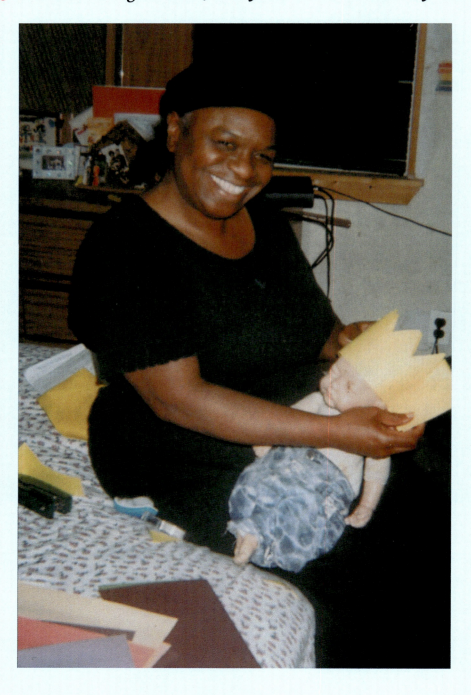

Even though God was King of the world: He came as a poor baby.

He was born in a stable

A king was trying to kill the poor baby King, but it was impossible to get the Christ *Jesus!*

The Lord was born on a special day!

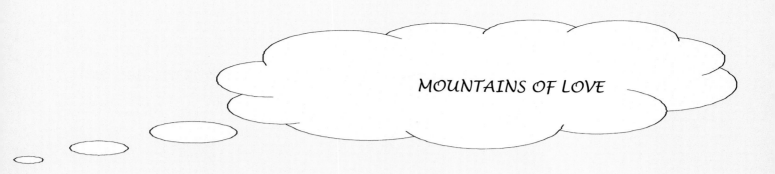

MOUNTAINS OF LOVE

The
Mountains By:
Barbara Ann Mary Mack
October 26, 2010

Mountains of Love: Sing in front of The Lord!

Sing! O Glorious Mountains of Love.

Melodies from Heaven
By: Barbara Ann Mary Mack
    October 27, 2010

Love everyone who gives and shares! Bless every person on Earth!
Mountains of Love: Mountains of Love: Sing!

Sing! O Mountains of Love: Sing!

HOLD ME! LORD *JESUS*

IN THE DARK: WILL YOU HOLD ME? O LORD!
IN THE MIDST OF EVIL: WILL YOU GUARD ME FROM THE GATES OF HELL?
WHEN TIME IS HARD: WILL YOU CALM ME WITH YOUR WARM ARMS OF LOVE?
MY HEART IS HOPING FOR THE WARMTH OF YOUR ARMS.
JESUS CHRIST: HOLD ME TIGHT!

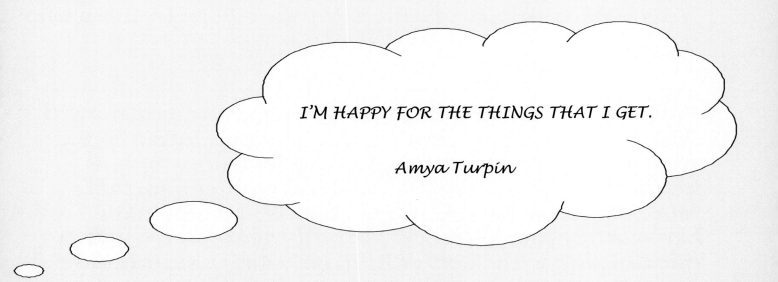

I'M HAPPY FOR THE THINGS THAT I GET.

Amya Turpin

READERS COMMENTS

Beautiful, lovely, short and to the point! I loved every word!

Alvena Johnson (Amya's great aunt)

Great job Amya!
"This book is inspiring and will infuse hope in those who read it." -

Kemi O

"Life" is an amazing and mature communication with God and "God's children". Amya Turpin's latest book of poems is a powerful free flowing testimony of how we can be human while maintaining a comfortable relationship with God. Amya reveals how she takes her relationship with God seriously while sharing this relationship with "God's Children". Amya enlightens us on how to delve in the pastoral with directness, enlightenment and passion. Amya has done it again; great writing so refreshing it challenges all of us to build a personal relationship with God!

Rudolph P. Ampofo, Philadelphia, PA

I am pleased to see that Amya is growing as a writer, and more importantly growing in her relationship with the Lord.

Barbara Paquette, Librarian

Spoken from the heart!
Dr. Pamela Huffman-Devaughn (Amya's doctor)

It was informative; and it gave me something to think about. It was written well for someone of that age. I would like to congratulate her for writing something to educate us.

Officer Joe Young, 12th Police District

Printed in the United States
by Baker & Taylor Publisher Services